Christian E

Master Chef of France

THE BEST RECIPES FROM PROVENÇAL COOKING

Acknowledgements

Hôtel de La Mirande
Les Olivades (Provençal fabrics)
Geneviève Lethu (crockery)
Terre è Provence (crockery)
Jaffier Parsi (matériel de cuisine)
Ferrari Fleurs (flowers)
All the market producers, and especially
Le Panier des Halles (fruit and vegetables)
M. Hugon (poultry)
M. Fenateau (fish)

Photographs: Didier BENAOUDA
Translation: Entreprises 35

Restaurant Christian Etienne
10, rue de Mons
Avignon

ÉDITIONS OUEST-FRANCE
13 rue du Breil, Rennes

Red Mullet with thick black-olive sauce

Introduction

Provençal cooking is without doubt one of the best of the "traditional" world. If proof is needed, when we read the menus of the great chefs of France and Navarre, we immediately discover the indisputable influence of our beautiful region: olive oil, thyme, garlic and other spices are used everywhere, and so much the better! The great cooks have always been ambassadors for a region, a territory, and even a culture.

As far as I am concerned, Provençal cooking is that of my childhood, with a mother who had cooked all her life. She taught me this love of work well done, which has a taste. The blue skies and all the odours of our *garrigues* can only accentuate the richness of our products: transforming them, cooking them, simmering them as simply as possible in order to keep all the authentic flavours.

And besides, Provence is bathed by the Mediterranean and has a border with Italy. So many peoples and cultures have settled in our region that the influence of navigators and invaders has evidently found its way onto our plates.

I would like to point out that our cooking has great character, with splendid savours and scents. Our dishes should have the perfume of our flowers, and should be as beautiful as our sun and our blue skies.

Poichichade

Provençal starters

Poichichade (Chick-pea soup)

For 6 to 8 persons

250 gm (8 oz) of cooked chick-peas, **2** or **3** crushed cloves of garlic, the juice of **2** lemons; **1** soup-spoon of olive oil, **1** pinch of paprika, salt, cayenne pepper to taste, **1** soup-spoon of chopped parsley, chicken stock

Put the chick-peas through the vegetable mixer, adding the lemon juice, crushed garlic, seasoning and the chicken stock so as to obtain a purée which is not too thick.

Reheat gently.

Serve in a big bowl, powder with paprika and chopped parsley.

Sprinkle with olive oil and grilled sesame seeds.

This dish is meant to start the meal, and is served with slices of toast and a good white wine.

Tapenade

For 6 to 8 persons

200 gm (6 oz) pulp of black olives, **50 gm** (1 1/2 oz) anchovy fillets, **50 gm** (1 1/2 oz) tuna marinated in oil, **100 gm** (3 oz) capers in vinegar, **1** to **2** spoonfuls of olive oil according to the consistency.

Use a pestle and mortar to crush the ingredients to a smooth paste. At the last minute, add the olive oil. Keep in a tightly-closed container.

Anchovy fillets (when in season)

For 6 to 8 persons

Lift the fillets from the bone, it is very easy! Anchovy fillets simply seasoned with lemon juice, olive oil, salt and pepper are a wonderful dish of great finesse.

If you have no fresh anchovies, you can follow the same recipe with anchovy fillets in salt, well washed and soaked in cold water for half a day. They will become much less salty and are eaten with cubes of toasted bread (croûtons).

In Provence the starter is a big event, and takes a lot of time. For us, it is almost a whole meal.

Tomato tartare with raw herbs and shallots, olive-oil vinaigrette

First course

Game "Caillettes"(little "quails" of game)

For 10 persons

500 gm (1 lb) game trimmings (such as hare or deer)
— this recipe is very suitable for the left-overs —
200 gm (6 oz) cooked spinach, **50 gm** (1 1/2 oz) cooked sorrel, **100 gm** (3 oz) finely sliced and cooked onions, **3** cloves of garlic, **100** to **150** gm (3 to 4 1/2 oz) pork membrane, thyme, bay leaves, sage

Dice the game finely and cook it for a long time as for a civet in order to obtain a fairly dry stuffing.

Make the stuffing with the spinach, onion, garlic, thyme and the game.

Roll it into little balls of about 30 gm (1 oz) in the membrane.

Place these in an oven-proof dish, half-covered with stock.

Place the sage and bay leaves on top and cook gently for 1 hour.

The caillettes (little quails) can be made with game, lamb or pork. They are perfect for a mid-morning snack and can be eaten hot or cold, accompanied by a salad and a white Lirac wine.

Pistou soup

100 gm (3 oz) big runner beans, **100 gm** (3 oz) white coco-beans,
2 or **3** courgettes, **100 gm** (3 oz) carrots, **50 gm** (1 1/2 oz) potatoes,
100 gm (3 oz) thick vermicelli, **4** very ripe tomatoes, **5** cloves of garlic,
1 bunch of basil, **75 gm** (2 oz) parmesan cheese,
25 cl (1/2 pint) olive oil, **2.5 l** (5 pints) water

Top and tail the runner beans, remove the strings, and cut them into pieces. Dice the courgettes.

Cook the coco-beans and runner beans in 5 pints of water, with salt and pepper. After 15 minutes, add the carrots and potatoes. 15 minutes later, add the courgettes.

Cook for another 15 minutes and then put in the vermicelli.

Crush the tomatoes into a pulp together with the skinned garlic, the parmesan cheese and the basil leaves, adding the oil little by little.

Pour into the soup while it is boiling.

This soup, which comes from Genoa, is served these days either hot in the autumn or cold in summer. The amount of tomatoes added determines how refreshing it is. Often a few pieces of bacon fat or slightly stale left-overs are added.

With a soup, it is best not to drink anything except the wonderful brew itself.

Tomato tartare with raw herbs and shallots, olive-oil vinaigrette

For 6 persons

10 big tomatoes, **1** shallot, **1** bunch of basil, Maussane olive-oil,
salt, pepper, balsamic vinegar

Blanch and peel the tomatoes, cut them into quarters and remove the pips. Press them for as long as possible. Rehydrate them with olive oil.

Season with salt and pepper, and add the chopped basil and thinly cut shallot plus several drops of balsamic vinegar.

To present, put into round moulds and sprinkle with olive oil just before serving.

This is a very simple dish. By pressing the tomatoes overnight, all their excess water disappears. When they are rehydrated with a fine quality olive oil, their flavour is even more delicate and pleasing, especially when well-ripened tomatoes have been selected.

I advise drinking a Côtes-du-Rhône 100% Viognier from M. Français (Château Saint-Estève d'Uchaux).

Iced fondant of tomatoes in a basil pulp

Iced fondant of tomatoes in a basil pulp

For 6 persons

1.5 kg (3 lbs) fresh tomatoes, **100 gm** (3 oz) whipped cream, **3** sheets of gelatine, **15 gm** (1/2 oz) tarragon, **15 gm** (1/2 oz) basil, **1** stalk of celery (about 1 1/2 oz), **6** pistils of saffron, **25 cl** (1/2 pint) of olive oil for the sauce, **30 gm** (1 oz) chopped basil, **1** sprig of thyme, **1** clove of garlic, **15 gm** (1/2 oz) sugar, **1** drop of Tabasco, milled salt and pepper.

Nick the tomatoes, put them in boiling water, peel them and cut them into big cubes. Reserve 250 gm (8 oz) for the sauce (coulis).

Peel the celery stalk and cut it into lengths of about 1/2 inch.

Put into a stew-pan: the diced tomatoes, the pieces of celery, the saffron, the thyme, the garlic and the sugar. Add a pinch of salt and a little pepper and cook without a lid for 1 hour, stirring from time to time.

Finely chop the tarragon and a little of the basil.

Soften the sheets of gelatine in cold water.

When the tomato coulis is ready, sieve it and measure the liquid obtained. You should have about 400 gm (12 oz). If you have too much, reduce it to the required amount.

Incorporate the drained gelatine into the very hot tomato coulis and mash it to make it dissolve. (If the tomato coulis is not hot enough, reheat it before adding the gelatine!).

Adjust the seasoning, add a drop of Tabasco, then the chopped tarragon and basil, and let it cool before incorporating the whipped cream.

Whip the cream and add to the tomato sauce, a fifth initially and then the rest delicately, turning the whole mixture and rotating the bowl. Leave it in the refrigerator for half a day, to set, in a suitable container.

Prepare the accompanying tomato coulis with the 8 oz of fresh tomatoes put aside. Season, incorporate the remaining basil and olive oil according to taste.

Turn out carefully onto the serving plate.

This dish, which is especially appreciated in summer, can be prepared 24 or even 48 hours in advance. It is very refreshing when the weather is hot. I suggest toasting several slices of country bread to give a little extra something.

As an accompaniment, I advise a rosé wine from the Ile de Porquerolles: Domaine de l'Alycastre.

Brandade of cod with truffles and garlic croûtons

For 10 to 15 persons

1 kg (2 lbs) of salted cod, **1 kg** (2 lbs) of fresh cod, **1 l** (2 pints) of milk, **1 l** (2 pints) of olive oil, **1** whole head of garlic, **1** baguette

Desalt the salted cod the previous day. Cut it in big dice, together with the fresh cod. Poach it in the milk with the fresh cod. Drain, then thicken with olive oil.

Using a spatula, stir vigorously at the edge of the heating ring, and add the olive oil until a homogeneous paste is obtained, with the consistency of a purée.

At the last minute, incorporate the garlic, crushed into a purée.

Season to taste (be careful with the salt).

Brandade of cod is one of the greatest specialities of Nîmes. Referring back to previous times, the inhabitants of Nîmes bartered salt with the sailors. This is why cod is a Nîmes speciality. In Vaucluse, we add truffles when they are in season, and this gives it a very special flavour. One can also add diced black olives, slightly grilled, and rubbed with garlic, which gives an extra taste.

I advise a fairly dry Côtes-du-Rhône with this dish, appelation Cairanne Villages (Domaine de l'Oratoire Saint-Martin-M. Alary).

Roasted cod steaks on a bed of ratatouille

FISH

Roasted cod steaks on a bed of ratatouille

1 fresh cod, **3 kg** (6 lbs), **1** onion, **1** red pepper,
1 green pepper, **3** courgettes,
2 aubergines, **3** cloves of garlic, **1** bouquet garni,
150 gm (4 1/2 oz) crushed tomatoes,
salt, pepper, olive oil

Fillet the cod and then take out the remaining bones. Cut six steaks from the thick part.

Rough-cut all the vegetables for the ratatouille, and keep apart.

Sauté the peppers, onion and the crushed garlic.

Pan the courgettes and aubergines separately in olive oil. Add them all together in a thick-bottomed pan with the peppers, onions, crushed tomatoes, and stew slightly. The vegetables should remain slightly crunchy.

Season to taste, then drain in order to collect the cooking juice and the oil.

Pan the slices of cod on the skin side, till they are crisp, and finish cooking in the oven.

Arrange the ratatouille in quenelles on the plate with the slice of cod.

Decorate with fried basil leaves.

Cod is an extraordinary fish. For this recipe, one should choose big pieces, since roasted fish is much better when it is thick.

I advise drinking a white AOC Palette - Château Simone from M. Rougier with this dish.

Stuffed Squids

12 small squids weighing 100 to 150 gm each (3 to 4 1/2 oz each), olive oil, **4** onions,
1/2 bunch of finely chopped parsley, **1/2** bunch of chives, **10 gm** (1/2 oz) tarragon,
100 gm (3 oz) diced peppers, **100 gm** (3 oz) pickled tomatoes, **2** cloves of garlic, chopped.

Separate the tentacles from the pouches, remove the skins from the pouches and rinse abundantly.

Dry, add salt and pepper.

Chop the tentacles, fry them gently in olive oil until brown.

Add the onions.

Blanch the diced peppers. Cook for 10 minutes, then add the parsley.

Stuff this mixture into the squid pouches and close both ends with wooden tooth-picks.

Cook in olive oil until they turn brown, or grill them on the barbecue.

Make a vinaigrette sauce with balsamic vinegar, add chopped black olives and herbs.

Serve with a few lettuce leaves.

Bouillabaisse

Bouillabaisse

For 10 persons

Fish soup

3 kg (6 lbs) "red soup", **1** leek, **1** fennel root,
3 garlic heads (cut in half), **1** onion,
250 gm (8 oz) tomato concentrate, thyme, bay leaves, a generous pinch of saffron.

Let the vegetables sweat without browning them. Add the fish (red soup), the tomato concentrate, the saffron. Mix thoroughly until the fish disintegrates.

Add water to cover.

Cook for 3 hours on moderate heat. Then sieve (not too fine a sieve).

Season with salt and pepper and keep warm. There should be at least 5 litres (10 pints) of soup.

Fish

5 average red mullets (200 gm : 6 oz each),
2 John Dory fillets (500 gm : 1 lb. each), cut into 10 portions,
5 weevers (100 gm : 3 oz each),
1 small conger eel (cut into pieces of about 80 gm : 2 1/2 oz each),
5 average scorpion fish - *rascasses*, (200 gm : 6 oz each),
5 red gurnets (200 gm : 6 oz each).

Take three wide frying pans. Put the red gurnets and the weevers in one; in another the rascasses and the red mullets; and the conger eel and the John Dory in the third.

Sprinkle the fish with olive oil and a little salt.

Then moisten half way up with the soup and begin to cook the fish. Once cooked, keep them warm.

Rouille

2 egg yolks,
50 cl (1 pint) olive oil,
3 cloves of garlic, a pinch of saffron, paprika, salt and cayenne pepper.

Crush the garlic finely then add the egg-yolks, a pinch of saffron, paprika, salt and cayenne pepper.

Add the oil, mixing gently as for a mayonnaise.

Soften with a soup-spoon of slightly reduced fish soup.

Other ingredients

200 gm (6 oz) of grated cheese,
1 baguette for croûtons, a few *rate* type potatoes boiled in water, slightly perfumed with saffron, for the garnish

First of all serve the remaining soup with the croûtons, the cheese and the rouille.

Next, present all the fish on a single platter with a little of the broth.

Many stories are told about this marvellous recipe and many regions interpret them differently. The recipe changes from village to village. But it is certain that, etymologically, the name comes from "quand ça boue, tu abaisse" (when it boils, you lower the heat).

Great names such as Morard, a Provençal chef with a great reputation, used the coral of sea-urchins in his rouille.

As far as I am concerned, any recipe is always a sheer pleasure, as long as it is prepared with love and passion and shared with good friends.

A good white wine from Cassis, or an AOC Bellet (a small vineyard above Nice) go perfectly with this dish.

Monkfish tail in breadcrumbs with its aïoli sauce

Sole stuffed with aubergine caviar

For 6 persons

6 soles of 200 to 250 gm (6 to 8 oz), trimmed, with both the white and black skin removed, **4** large aubergines, **25 gm** (3/4 oz) pine kernels and grilled almonds, **1** onion, **3** cloves of garlic, **50 cl** (1 pint) white wine, **25 cl** (1/2 pint) olive oil, thyme, a bay leaf, salt, pepper.

Put the aubergines in the oven to cook with the thyme and bay leaf.

Make an aubergine caviar mixture, adding a little olive oil to obtain a rich and smooth paste.

Fry the soles in butter (meunière) making sure that they remain pink near the bone.

Fillet the soles.

Reconstitute them, replacing the bone by the aubergine caviar.

Place them on a serving dish.

Reheat them in a slow oven, sprinkled with a little olive oil.

This dish can be served on generous slices of grilled tomatoes.

I advise drinking a well structured white wine with this recipe, Hermitage style or a light red wine such as the Rasteau Rabasse Charavin from Corinne Couturier.

Red Mullet with thick black-olive sauce

For 6 persons

6 red mullet of 200 to 300 gm, (6 to 9 oz) each, **300 gm** (9 oz) black olives, **25 cl** (1/2 pint) Noilly Prat, **25** cl (1/2 pint) fresh cream, **200 gm** (6 oz) butter, olive oil

Remove the bones from the red mullets.

Blanch the olives and cook them with the Noilly Prat and a little of the cream. Mix.

Sieve and add the butter to thicken.

Fry the red mullet quickly in olive oil.

The difficulty with this recipe is preparing the fillets. If you are among friends and they don't mind eating with their fingers, leave the bones and simply enjoy yourselves.

For the sauce, it is advisable to choose Greek olives rather than those of Nyons, since they are not so oily.

I advise drinking a white wine from the Luberon as accompaniment, Château La Verrerie or Val Joanis.

Monkfish tail in breadcrumbs with its aïoli sauce

For 2 persons

1 tail of monkfish of 800 gm to 1 kg (1 1/2 to 2 lbs), **300 gm** (10 oz) breadcrumbs, **20 gm** (3/4 oz) thyme flowers, olive oil, **6** cloves of garlic, **2** eggs, **100 gm** (3 oz) butter.

Skin and trim the monkfish, insert several cloves of garlic and cover it with breadcrumbs mixed with thyme flowers.

Cook gently in olive oil and butter.

Cook in the oven at 180°C, basting often with the olive oil and butter.

For the sauce, crush the garlic with a pestle and mortar and a pinch of coarse salt.

When the paste is thick and smooth, add the egg yolks.

Incorporate the olive oil little by little.

Continue adding until the desired quantity is obtained.

Take the monkfish out of the oven, and put it in a serving dish. The aïoli sauce is served separately.

One can also prepare this recipe with small tails of monkfish, counting one per person. This fish can be accompanied by any boiled vegetable, such as potatoes, carrots and celery hearts.

I advise drinking a white Côtes-du-Rhône Villages (at least two years old) with this dish; Château Saint-Roch from M. Verda (Laudun).

Amandine
LIQUEUR
Alc. 25% vol.
Farigoule
LIQUEUR
Alc. 40% vol.
PASTIS
HB
HENRI BARDOUIN
350 ml
43% vol.
Trigolet
1981
MIEL de LAVANDES
M. MUSSATO
84110 ROAIX
1 kg.
de Provence & Dauphiné

La Coupo Santo
18 67
La Coupo Santo di Felibre
Paroles de Frédéric MISTRAL
Harmonisation de Michel FLORET
Modéré
Prouvençau, veici la Coupo
Que nous vèn di Catalan :
A-de-rèng beguen en troupo
Lou vin pur de noste plant,
D'un vièi pople fièr e libre
Sian bessai la finicioun ;
E, se toumbon li Felibre,
Toumbara nosto nacioun.
D'uno raço que regrèio
Sian bessai li proumié grèu :
Sian bessai de la patrìo
Li cepoun emai li priéu.
Vuejo-nous lis esperanço
E li raive dóu jouvènt,
Dóu passat la remembranço,
E la fe dins l'an que vèn.
Vuejo nous la couneissènço
Dóu Verai emai dóu Bèu,
MALLARD

MEAT

Daube, Avignon style

For 6 to 8 persons

Cut up a boned leg of lamb into cubes weighing about 90 gm (3 oz).

Push a small piece of bacon seasoned with spicy salt into each cube along the grain of the meat.

Marinade the pieces of lamb for 2 hours with: 10 cl (1/4 pint) of oil per litre (2 pints) of wine, sliced carrots and onions, 4 cloves of garlic, thyme, bay leaves and parsley, plus 1 stick of celery.

Prepare 3 chopped onions mixed with 2 crushed cloves of garlic.

Blanch 250 gm (8 oz) fatty bacon finely diced.

Cut 250 gm (8 oz) fresh bacon rind into 1 inch squares, then blanch them.

Prepare a bunch of parsley around a dried orange peel.

Line the base and sides of a terrine with thin bacon-fat slices (*barde*), then fill with the pieces of lamb in layers, alternating with the onions, the bacon and rind, sprinkling each layer of meat with powdered thyme and bay leaves.

Place the bunch of parsley in the middle of the terrine, and season each layer lightly.

Moisten with the sieved marinade, close the terrine, and seal down the lid hermetically with a flour and water paste in order to ensure that it does not dry out.

Then place it in the oven, and cook gently for 5 hours at a constant temperature.

To serve, open the terrine, take off the *bardes*, pour off the grease and remove the bunch of parsley.

The daube should be served as such, in its cooking terrine.

This is a recipe which takes a long time, and which our ancestors cooked in the chimney, but if you have time and love dishes cooked in sauce, this recipe is a sheer delight.

This dish merits a vintage red Côtes-du-Rhône. You can drink the same wine you used for cooking.

Roast loin of lamb with courgettes and tomatoes

For 6 persons

2 loins (*carrés*) of lamb of 1 to 1.2 kg each - about 2 lbs each (it is a good idea to ask your butcher if you can keep the bones when he prepares them, since you can use these for the juice),
6 courgettes, **8** tomatoes, **3** onions, **8** cloves of garlic, thyme, bay leaves.

Prepare a juice with the lamb bones: brown them in the oven, and then put them in the casserole with garlic, onion, thyme and bay leaves.

Cook gently for 2 hours, then sieve and reduce again, skimming all the time.

Separately, prepare the vegetables. Slice the courgettes and the tomatoes thinly. Place the courgettes and the tomatoes in an oven-proof dish on a bed of chopped onions sprinkled with thyme, bay leaves and crushed garlic, layer by layer. Pour over a little olive oil and place in a hot oven (150 to 160°C - about 320°F) for 2 hours, covered with aluminium paper and a lid so that all the flavours mix together.

An hour before the meal, cook the lamb till it is pink, 20 minutes in a very hot oven is quite enough (180 to 200°C - about 380°F).

Let the meat stand a little, and then reheat it slightly before serving with the courgettes and tomatoes, using your tasty juice to moisten everything.

Daube, Avignon style

Cake of aubergines with lamb "panoufles", braised with tomatoes pickled in wine

For 8 persons

1.2 kg (2 1/2 lbs) neck of lamb, boned (keep the bones for the juice), **8** completely ripe tomatoes, **6** big well-ripened aubergines, **2** courgettes, **1** head of garlic, **2** big onions, **1** glass of dry white wine, thyme, bay leaves, olive oil, salt, milled pepper.

Prepare a sauté of lamb with the meat, and a juice from the bones.

Brown the pieces of meat and add the onions and garlic.

Dice the courgettes and tomatoes and add the white wine.

Cook gently for 2 hours.

Slice the aubergines finely, lengthways, and fry them in olive oil. Then line small round moulds (to serve individually) or a shallow gratin dish.

Place the ragoût in the middle and cover with the remaining aubergine slices.

Finish the cooking on a gentle heat, for another 30 minutes.

Serve with the juice from the lamb, blending in several cloves of garlic, crushed finely into a paste.

This very economical and very tasty recipe can also be made with the leftovers of cooked lamb.

I advise drinking a white Châteauneuf-du-Pape. A recent vintage would be excellent, for example a Vieux Télégraphe from the Brunier family.

* Panoufle : a piece constituted of the fat and muscle covering the floating ribs.

Trotters and packets

12 little lamb packets (*paquets*), **6** sheep's trotters, **1** pepper, **1 kg** (2 lbs) tomatoes, **200 gm** (6 oz) carrots, **300 gm** (9 oz) onions, **1** litre (2 pints) white wine.

The packets are made of lamb tripes cut into triangles, stuffed with a big lump of salted pork and a parsley, garlic and breadcrumbs mixture (persillade), rolled and tied with string. Personally, I would advise you to ask your tripe butcher to do this.

Let the vegetables sweat in a little olive oil. When they are well coloured, add the trotters and then the packets on top. Add the tomatoes last, with salt, pepper and pimento.

Moisten with 2 pints of good white wine and complete with water if necessary.

Cook for 6 hours in a slow oven. Once cooked, remove the packets and trotters.

Re-cook the sauce so that it is no longer acid. This dish is served very hot with boiled potatoes.

This is a splendid Provençal recipe. There is always a celebration when someone in the family prepares this dish. It is often a pretext for inviting friends, since it is a meal meant for sharing.

I advise drinking a light Côtes-du-Rhône red wine: Domaine de la Remejeanne from M. and Mme. Klein, winegrowers who are as enthusiastic as myself.

Trotters and packets

Saddle of rabbit with pistou

For 6 persons

3 boned saddles of rabbit, salted and peppered and rolled in their "panoufles", with a sprig of rosemary, **1** onion, **10** basil leaves, **4** cloves of garlic, **25 cl** (1/2 pint) white wine, **2** grains of coriander, **1** bouquet garni, salt, pepper, **30** to **50 gm** (1 to 1 1/2 oz) butter.

Sauté the saddles in a thick-bottomed frying pan, with their bones and the onion.

Cook in a very hot oven for 15 to 20 minutes.

Once they are cooked, take them out and let them rest.

Degrease the frying pan, add the white wine and an equal amount of water to the bones.

Add the bouquet garni, the garlic and the coriander.

Cook gently until the liquid is reduced by half.

Sieve this sauce, add the butter little by little and the basil at the last minute.

Cut the saddles in half.

One can serve this dish with white coco-beans or French beans.

This is a most refreshing dish, and quick to prepare. It is full of flavour. A red Côtes-du-Rhône, Coteau-des-Baux, or a Château Romanin accompanies it very well.

Roast partridge in a cabbage "chartreuse"

For 4 persons

2 partridges, **1** curly cabbage, **2** finely-chopped onions, **2** finely-chopped carrots, **100 gm** (3 oz) salted pork, diced, **5** cloves of garlic

Cut the cabbage in four. Take out the central wedges and keep the green leaves on one side. Blanch in boiling water and cool rapidly.

Start braising the white leaves with the onions and carrots and the pork, after letting it sweat. Leave to cook for 2 hours in an oven at 130-150°C (about 280°F).

Roast the partridges with the cloves of garlic, 5 minutes on each side and 5 minutes on the back. Let them rest for 10 minutes, bone them, keep the breasts in the fatty juice which has come from the birds. The thighs are probably rather pink, so grill them a little.

Break up the carcass and simmer to prepare a good stock, barely covering it with water. Cook until only half the liquid remains, sieve and keep aside.

During this time, make a cabbage chartreuse using a little circular mould 5 cm (2 ins) in diameter and 3 to 4 cm (about 1 1/2 ins) high. Line the moulds with the very green cabbage leaves and fill with the mixture. Braise and re-cook in a hot oven (150-160°C: about 300°F) for 30 minutes.

Place the partridge breasts in the centre of the serving dish, with the thighs around them and the hot juice.

Drink a good Châteauneuf-du-Pape or red Gigondas with this dish.

Saddle of rabbit with pistou

Vegetables

Tomatoes Provençal

Olive oil, chopped parsley, breadcrumbs,
10 chopped cloves of garlic, **1.5 kg** (3 lbs) tomatoes.

Cut the tomatoes in two horizontally and empty out the seeds. Place them on a plate.

Mix the garlic, parsley and breadcrumbs to make a persillade.

Cover the tomatoes with this mixture.

Pour olive oil over the tomatoes.

Place in a hot oven for 10 to 15 minutes, depending on the size of the tomatoes.

Reduce the cooking juice and add a few drops of vinegar. This sauce is a wonderful accompaniment to your tomatoes Provençal.

This is a very easy recipe. When the season comes, every house in Provence has a plate of tomatoes ready, cooked this way. They can be eaten cold. When hot, they go very well with grilled lamb.

I advise drinking a Tavel with this dish, a very structured rosé which harmonises perfectly.

Small stuffed tomatoes with savours of tarragon

For 6 persons

18 small round tomatoes, **2 kg** (4 lbs) marmandes tomatoes, **10** tarragon leaves,
25 cl (1/2 pint) beef stock, **2** cloves of garlic, **1** onion

Blanch the little tomatoes, cut off the top third horizontally to form a cap, and remove the pips. Turn them upside down to empty out the juice.

Crush the marmandes (blanch, remove the pips, cut into pieces).

Let the onion and the cloves of garlic sweat in olive oil with the crushed marmande tomatoes.

Continue cooking until all the juice has gone.

Add the chopped tarragon leaves and stuff the tomatoes.

Cook for 5 minutes in a hot oven with the beef stock and serve immediately.

The interest of this recipe is that it brings out the real taste of tomato. For a maximum of flavour, the tomatoes to be stuffed must be less ripe and firmer than the marmandes to be crushed.

I advise a white Laudun Villages, from the Quatre-Chemins co-operative.

Artichokes stuffed the Provençal way with basil
("en barigoule"*)

For 6 personnes

12 purple artichokes, **2** carrots, **2** onions, **4** cloves of garlic, **1** stick of celery, **1** bunch of basil, **100 gm** (3 oz) salted pork, olive oil, thyme, bay leaves, white stock.

Turn the artichokes, removing the green and hard leaves with a small knife.

Cut off the tender leaves at the level of the choke and keep them aside.

Remove the choke with a small spoon.

Chop finely the carrots, onions, celery and salted pork.

Slice the tender leaves and the base of the artichokes.

Let the pieces of salted pork sweat until they start to brown. Add the carrots, onions, artichoke leaves, and cook until the mixture is dry.

Moisten to mid-height with a little of the stock.

Cook for 5 to 10 minutes depending on the size.

Let the mixture stand for several hours.

If you have a lot of juice remaining after cooking, reduce it a little and adjust the seasoning. Add a few drops of olive oil and the chopped basil.

Serve very hot.

This dish can also be served cold with a vinaigrette sauce made with the juice, and can be eaten as an accompaniment to many sorts of grilled fish.

As for the wine, I suggest a red Ventoux, Château La Croix-des-Pins from M. Avon.

*Barigoule : from "*barigoulo*", the Provençal word for field mushrooms or other mushrooms.

Tomatoes Provençal

Ratatouille

6 courgettes, **2** onions, **3** green peppers, **6** tomatoes, **3** cloves of garlic, **4** aubergines, **1** big bouquet garni

Cut the courgettes into cubes without peeling them.

Peel and slice up the onions.

Empty the peppers and dice them.

Peel, remove the pips and cut the tomatoes into quarters.

Crush the garlic.

Strip the aubergines and cut them into big cubes.

Fry the aubergines and courgettes in a frying pan, put them in a colander for their oil to drip.

Blanch the peppers in plenty of water.

Let the onions sweat in a little oil and almost brown them.

Mix everything together (onions, tomatoes, aubergines, courgettes, peppers and the garlic last).

Add the bouquet garni and bring to the boil.

Add salt and pepper, and it's ready.

Ratatouille, the famous Provençal recipe, can be eaten hot or cold. It is traditional not to peel the vegetables since the skin adds flavour and the vegetables do not end up as a purée. Evidently, it is advisable to wash them well and to use fresh products from the markets of Provence.

Ragoût of snow-peas with bacon

For 8 to 10 persons

1 kg (2 lbs) snow peas (mangetout), **100 gm** (3 oz) diced fresh bacon, **2** onions, **4** cloves of garlic, **50 cl** (1 pint) beef stock or water, **5 cl** (1/10 pint) olive oil, **50 gm** (1 1/2 oz) pickled tomatoes, salt, pepper

Brown the bacon and chopped onions in the olive oil.

Add the garlic and sugar peas with 1 pint of beef stock and cook gently for 10 minutes.

Season with salt and pepper.

Arrange the mixture in a circle and pour the reduced beef juice in the centre, with the diced pickled tomatoes around the edge.

Previously, green vegetables were cooked in large quantities of water; sugar peas and spinach for example. These days, it is more usual to braise them gently so that they give their own juice and remain aromatic. The result is better, and the vitamins are conserved as well.

I suggest drinking a Châteauneuf-du-Pape or a red Bandol.

Ragoût of snow-peas with bacon

Desserts

Fennel sorbet with saffron sauce

For 8 to 10 persons

950 gm (2 lbs) sugar, **2 l** (4 pints) water, **100 gm** (3 oz) glucose, **500 gm** (1 lb) fennel seeds, **1** spoonful of honey

Make a syrup with the sugar, water, glucose and honey. Add the fennel seeds and let everything infuse for several hours. Rotate in the sorbet freezer.

Prepare a custard slightly perfumed with saffron.

This dessert is very pleasant when served with spiced bread or a *trou normand* of several drops of Pastis.

Pine-kernel tart

For 6 to 8 persons

Tart base in sweet pastry, **100 gm** (3 oz) sugar, **100 gm** (3 oz) butter, **400 gm** (12 oz) pine kernels, **25 cl** (1/2 pint) double cream.

Prepare a light brown caramel with the butter. Add the pine kernels. Let them cook and then add the cream to make a sauce. Pour into the tart base. Cook in the oven.

This is a very typical Provençal recipe; the pine kernels can be replaced by chopped almonds, and the tart remains soft for at least two days.

I suggest drinking a vintage Muscat de Beaumes-de-Venise with this, coming from the co-operative cellars.

Croquants ("crunchies")

For 8 to 10 persons

400 gm (12 oz) flour, **250 gm** (8 oz) whole almonds (with the skin), **125 gm** (4 oz) icing sugar, **4** eggs, salt

Mix the flour, sugar and almonds. Stir in the eggs.

Roll little sausages about 20 mm (nearly 1 inch) in diameter.

Cook in the oven at 180°C (350°F) for 15 minutes. Cut into rounds when they are still hot.

A dry cake to be eaten at coffee-time or as a snack, a cake which grandmothers always keep in their cupboards.

Pine-kernel tart

Iced nougat with honey from Provence

125 gm (4 oz) sliced almonds, **50 gm** (1 1/2 oz hazelnuts), **25 gm** (3/4 oz) pistachio nuts, **200 gm** (6 oz) sugar, **100 gm** (3 oz) sultanas, **75 cl** (1 1/2 pints) whipped cream, **350 gm** (11 oz) honey, **75 gm** (2 oz) glucose, **250 gm** (8 oz) egg whites.

Grill the almonds, hazelnuts and pistachios.

Make a caramel with 150 gm (4 1/2 oz) sugar, and add the almonds. Turn onto a plate to cool.

Reduce to a powder, then grind up the hazelnuts and pistachios and add them.

Whip up the cream till it holds.

Make the honey meringue by heating the honey, the glucose and the rest of the sugar to 120°C (240°F).

Whip the egg-whites until they are completely firm and add the cooked honey. Mix until it is completely cooled down.

Mix the nougatine powder into the meringue. Add the sultanas.

Add the whipped cream.

Keep in the deep freeze.

Oreillettes ("ear flaps")

For 8 to 10 persons

1 kg (2 lbs) flour, salt, **250 gm** (8 oz) sugar, **20 gm** (1/2 oz) chemical yeast, **250 gm** (8 oz) soft butter, **8** eggs, orange flower extract

Mix the butter and sugar until they are smooth. Gradually add the flour and yeast.

Incorporate the eggs.

Flavour with orange flower extract.

Roll out the resulting paste, cut into rectangles and fry them in hot oil.

Powder with icing sugar.

Oreillettes are small fried cakes which we eat traditionally at Christmas. They are part of the Thirteen Desserts, and are particularly appreciated by children.

Provençal navettes ("bobbins")

750 gm (1 1/2 lbs) flour, **375 gm** (3/4 lb) powdered sugar, **65 gm** (2 oz) butter, salt, the zest of **1** lemon, **3** eggs, **10 cl** (1/5 pint) water

Make a hollow in the flour and add the sugar, the softened butter, the lemon zest, a pinch of salt and the eggs.

Incorporate the water to obtain a smooth paste.

Form little sausage shapes depending on the required size of the navettes.

Cut them into sections and make them oval in shape.

Place them on a buttered baking sheet.

Nick the centre of each navette.

Leave them to stand for 1 hour.

Brush them with egg yolk and then put them in a moderate oven.

Take them out when they are brown.

Oreillettes

List of Recipes

 - I.S.B.N 2 7373.2380.0 - Dépôt légal : mars 1998 - N° d'éditeur : 3768.01.02.03.98
Imprimerie Raynard, La Guerche-de-Bretagne (35).